Isley Lynn

SKIN A CAT

OBERON BOOKS
LONDON

WWW.OBERONBOOKS.COM

First published in 2016 by Oberon Books Ltd
521 Caledonian Road, London N7 9RH
Tel: +44 (0) 20 7607 3637 / Fax: +44 (0) 20 7607 3629
e-mail: info@oberonbooks.com
www.oberonbooks.com

A catalogue record for this book is available from the British Library.

PB ISBN: 9781786820525
E ISBN: 9781786820532

Cover Photo by Richard Lakos
Cover Design by Luke W. Robson

THANKS

To Playdate (CA, PC, SK, SL, VP, DR) and Crowther
Club (JB, SH, AW) for letting me sob on their shoulders
and always being first in the ticket line. To Inua Ellams and
Leo Butler for knowing the value of a good quote from
a good name. To Tell Tales (EK, FK, GM) and IdeasTap
Takeover: Love (GB, FF, SK, GM, KPW) for helping me
test sex on stage. To Blythe Stewart for immediately and
completely getting the play, and being the first to put her
money where her mouth was. To the SAC Creatives (JA,
JC, ID, LL, RL, HP, ZAR, HR, BS) who put literal blood
sweat and tears into the production. To Peggy Ramsay for
providing writers with serious support without bullshit.
To Vinay Patel for the big bucks. To the private donors
that got us up and running. To the Vault Festival for being
a genuine hub of genuine risk taking (and for the cool
award). To all the play's early champions (SG, LK, NT,
CW) for buzz and boost. To Jonathan Kinnersley for being
an incredible ally. To the NHS for making everything
within reach. To Marie Stopes for the play's ending. To
my parents and brother who understand the need to make
space for difference. To my family for inexhaustible love
and pride and support. To all the friends and all the lovers
who made it into this play (and those that didn't) for their
overwhelming acceptance. And to Geoffrey for everything,
all of it, every single bit.

Note on the Text

My experience of sex never matched up with what I saw in film, television, books, or the stage. Particularly where virginity was concerned, I was baffled as to how all the drama was in the lead up to the act, but not during. For me it had been the opposite. Not sexy. Not fun. Not what I expected or was taught would happen if I'd chosen the right dude to Do It with. I remember watching the movie Kinsey with my first proper boyfriend and both of us leaning forward in our seats when the primary couple is told by their doctor that there's a solution for their painful intercourse, but of course the camera cut straight to a blissful and giggling post-coitus, with no detail about what they'd done to achieve it (and of course frantic Googling afterwards wasn't fruitful either). So in a way this play is the missing part of the film I wished I'd seen at 16. Almost a decade later I figured that if we still weren't talking about how uneasy sex could be for some people (a surprising number in fact) then I probably should.

So I did. The whole play was very easy to write, but the script still suffered from what I now think was symptomatic of the story it told – I sent it to every venue and company I could, and most feedback was geared towards making the play something different to what it was, making it more like other plays. But I was by this point very clear that the whole point was that this play was not and should not be like other plays, because this story was not like other stories, and that's why it was important to me to tell it. When Blythe Stewart read it and immediately understood this I practically fell over myself in begging her to direct it. This turned out to be a smart move, because with grit, favours, our own bank accounts, our own bedding as set and the costume designer's own bra in the costume, we brought *Skin A Cat** to the Vault Festival, sold out every night, and were given the Pick Of The Year Award before being offered the opening slot of the brand new Bunker Theatre.

I wish I could tell my 15-25 year old self that one day all this horrible vagina stuff was going to make a great play that people would praise and thank me for (praise is really the only reason I do anything). But more than that I wish I could have known then what I know now – that I was not alone, and that it would be ok. I'm very honoured to be able to, through jokes about willies and bums and flaps, tell other Alanas out there that it's going to be ok.

*One of the weirdest reactions I've ever received to telling someone about the particulars of my sex life was from one of my ex-boyfriend's mother, who responded with caring nonchalance: "Well there's more than one way to skin a cat". I'd never heard that phrase before and it took some explaining, but it was (in so many ways) perfect.

'We are the only authority on what is good for us. Once we see this, we feel an enormous peace and freedom.'

Hugh Prather

'You alone are enough.'

Maya Angelou

Characters

ALANA: ages 9-25, played by someone 25 or older, very plain

MOTHER: Alana's mother

JESS: 15

SIMON: 17

KEVIN: 19

NATHANIEL: 16

PETER: 16-19

SALLY: 18-23

JOHNNY: 18-23

MARK: 20s

DOCTOR: female, 30s

GERRY: 50s

WAITRESS: 20s

PSYCHIATRIST: female, 40

SUGGESTED DOUBLING: Alana plays herself, one actor plays all male characters, one actor plays all female characters

A NOTE

This play is unashamedly autobiographical. That said, not all of it is true. I'll happily answer any questions that come up with regards to its staging, production, etc. Please don't hesitate to ask them.

KEY

/ marks the point of interruption in overlapping dialogue

… at the end of a line indicates a trailing off

… at the start of a line indicates thought about what is about to be said

– at the end of a line indicates an abrupt halt

If a character's line ends with– and their next lines begins with – then the lines run on as one without pause

(?) indicates a question that is not genuine

[ ] indicates speech which is not said out loud but is included to clarify the intention of the line

for Geoffrey
and myself

A bed.

ALANA enters, sees the bed.

ALANA: *(To the audience.)* Oh, this is – I thought – no I guess that's a cliché.

(Sits.)

Comfy. We won't have to... will we? No, good, ok then. Lovely. Sorry, I'm... nervous. But I'm, fully up for it. Definitely. And look just before I get started I just wanted to say something. I want to... This is really hard for me. This is what I've spent the last – a long time – ... this is basically my worst nightmare. Um. But I'm going to try. Because I think it's a good idea. So I'll just – [start]? Shall I?

I'm going to try and tell you everything. I'm going to try.

Ok. Um. Right.

I don't actually know where to start...

Yes I do.

MOTHER: Excuse me, do you have a pad on you? A sanitary pad? No? Thank you. Excuse me, you don't happen to have a pad on you? For women? I'm sorry, excuse me, I'm trying to get hold of a pad – feminine emergency. No, a tampon won't do I'm afraid. Thanks anyway. Excuse me, I'm sorry to interrupt, I was just wondering if anyone in your party had a pad, like a sanitary pad? No? Would you mind asking around? No no, I really need a pad.

ALANA: My mum's on holiday, on an island resort, and she's trying to find someone, anyone with a pad she can use. It's not for her. It's for me, back at the cabin with a folded wad of toilet paper wedged into my pants. I'm nine years old, and I'm having my first period.

I don't remember how I discovered it exactly... I remember the chaos that followed. Dad wasn't there. I mean, ever, he wasn't around. Never met him, and never wanted to, really. Easier. I figured if he hadn't been in touch he obviously didn't want to be. Or maybe he was dead. Anyway eventually one of the dive masters gave her some and by the next day they had all pooled their resources and come up with a rainbow of different brands for me to use. I thought that was fun, at first. But then I realized that my becoming a woman was ruining my mum's holiday a bit.

We did not talk about it. I had no idea what was going on. I felt very – wrong. Very bad. Why was this happening? Was I sick? Was I broken? Why wouldn't Mum talk to me? Why didn't she want anyone else talking to me either? Why did she look at her menu so much, out at the sea so much, at me so little? Why did she finish the books she brought so quickly? I was left to figure it all out by myself.

MOTHER: No more swimming.

ALANA: That's all she told me. So I studied what was left on the scratchy pads every few hours – red blood, yes, but brown too, and sometimes like clumps of jam. Sometimes little stringy aliens, stranded on the padding. They looked like biro marks, when you're not really writing you're just thinking, or on the telephone – my mum does that a lot, doodling her conversation. But now, she was silent and her hands were very still.

I thought this was going to be the way things were, forever, from here on out. I'll be bleeding for the rest of my life. I thought I'd never see my friends again. I thought maybe I was a witch – and that was a little exciting at first, I'll admit, but not after the first few days.

Thankfully, it stopped. Then started. Then stopped again and started again and I ruined a few good dresses before my mum sat on my bed with me and said:

MOTHER: It's called getting your period.

ALANA: *(To MOTHER.)* What is it?

MOTHER: It's menstruation.

ALANA: What's that?

MOTHER: It's natural.

ALANA: Oh.

MOTHER: Everybody does it.

ALANA: Everybody?

MOTHER: Every girl.

ALANA: Boys?

MOTHER: Not boys.

ALANA: Not boys?

MOTHER: No.

ALANA: Weird.

MOTHER: So there's nothing to worry about. –

ALANA: But / …

MOTHER: – It's perfectly fine, bound to happen one day. –

ALANA: But / …

MOTHER: – You were just early, of course.

ALANA: But what's happening?

MOTHER: *(Sighs.)* Inside you – there are – you know where eggs come from?

ALANA: Chickens?

MOTHER: Yes, well, you're / …

ALANA: I've got chickens?

MOTHER: No, you're like a chicken.

ALANA: No I'm not.

MOTHER: Because you've got eggs too.

ALANA: … What?

MOTHER: Inside you.

ALANA: *(Beat.)* How do we get them out?

MOTHER: They're coming out now.

ALANA: In the – ?

MOTHER: Yes.

ALANA: Doesn't look like eggs.

MOTHER: That's because they're so tiny you can't see them.

ALANA: But why am I bleeding?

MOTHER: Because – because every egg has a little cushion,
and when it comes out it takes the cushion with it and
that's where all the blood comes from.

ALANA: Like a water bed.

MOTHER: Exactly.

ALANA: *(To the audience.)* I had been begging for a water bed.

(To MOTHER.) Can't I just – keep them inside?

MOTHER: No.

ALANA: Why not.

MOTHER: You just can't.

ALANA: But why can't I?

MOTHER: Because then you'd be full of eggs!

ALANA: I don't mind.

MOTHER: Look – those eggs, if they stay in there, they go bad.

ALANA: Why?

MOTHER: Because they don't turn into babies.

ALANA: Babies?!

MOTHER: That's where babies come from, there, you might as
well know.

ALANA: Why don't they turn into babies?

MOTHER: You don't want babies do you.

ALANA: Why not!

MOTHER: Because then you'd have to give birth!

ALANA: Birth?

MOTHER: Oh my god, look, I'll buy you a book.

ALANA: *(To the audience.)* And that was that. And that was
all. But now, at least, I knew: I was normal, I was full of
eggs, and they wouldn't turn into babies. That was some
reassurance.

I started to notice... lots of things. All at once it was like
my legs, boobs, hips, shoulders, everything was ballooning
out. More new dresses. I spent a lot of time looking in the
mirror. I don't know how much is normal, but I'm pretty
sure, mine was too much. But I tried to avoid...

(She indicates her vagina.)

It was the ugliest thing I'd ever seen! In my life! No
wonder it's so hard to get a look at, who would want to
see that every day! I don't know how it had escaped my
attention until this point, but now I really took it all in
and I was suddenly deeply embarrassed that my mother
had seen such an awful, gross, flappy part of me. Had
interacted with it, had washed it and wiped it and streaked
it with ointment, had intimate knowledge of its wrinkles
and folds... And I was ashamed that I had let her do it.

I started locking the toilet door. Mum removed the lock.
I hated her for that. I hated her for a lot of things. I think
most girls do, isn't that right? Their mothers, not my
mother, not everyone hates my mother, just me.

Look I'm going to jump ahead a bit here because I didn't
have my first boyfriend until I was 15 because my best
friend was gorgeous, big boobs on top of skinny ribs so
when we were out together no one paid attention to me.

JESS: Guess what.

ALANA: *(To JESS.)* What?

JESS: Guess.

ALANA: No.

JESS: Go on.

ALANA: I don't know, you've given up smoking.

JESS: I had sex with Si.

ALANA: What!

JESS: Yeah.

ALANA: What like full sex?

JESS: Full sex.

ALANA: What was it like?

JESS: Incredible. I came four times. I think I'm a nymphomaniac.

ALANA: *(To the audience.)* She was lying. About the orgasms. It was so obvious she was lying. I knew it, at the time, I knew she was lying but I believed her anyway.

(To JESS.) Did it hurt?

JESS: Hurt? No! Of course not it was the best thing ever.

ALANA: But it hurts apparently, the first time.

JESS: Well it didn't.

ALANA: Not even a little bit?

JESS: I used to do horse riding, so.

ALANA: Alright but, I don't know I just thought it would, hurt. You know, stretching enough so much you fit someone else inside of you. When you've never done it before.

JESS: … Yeah ok. Yeah a bit.

(Beat.)

Keep a secret?

ALANA: Yeah.

JESS: … A lot. Actually. Blood. Don't tell anyone.

ALANA: *(To the audience.)* My first boyfriend, if I can call him that, he was actually her boyfriend. That, boyfriend. Si. Short for Simon. I never told her but maybe I think she knows now, I'm not sure, but at the time she didn't and I felt awful, just awful. But when your best friend's boyfriend comes up to you and says –

SIMON: You're pretty.

ALANA: *(To the audience.)* What do you do?

SIMON: Prettier than Jessie.

ALANA: *(To the audience.)* What do you even do?

SIMON: Can I have your number?

ALANA: *(To the audience.)* I was 15. No one had ever asked me for my number before. Or said I was pretty. And friends don't count, because they're just making you feel better for being the last one in the year to get a proper kiss, everyone knows that. But. This was the guy who had just made my best friend bleed – by default, really, my only friend really – my Only Friend.

(To SIMON.) Sure.

SIMON: Cool. I'll prank you.

ALANA: *(To the audience.)* I thought maybe he was just gathering info, you know, research for when they break up, who's available, who's up for it. Laying foundations, I don't know. But two days later he texts me, asking me if I wanted to see Bruce Almighty with him that weekend.

I knew for a fact he and Jess had not broken up.

I said yes.

He bought himself a popcorn. He did ask if I wanted a bit. I said alright. It was sweet and I like salty but I didn't mind. And we watched the film. And I was just bringing a huge handful to my mouth when –

SIMON kisses her suddenly.

ALANA: I will not call it kissing. I mean, come on. I dropped all the popcorn on the floor. And I didn't give a fuck. Then at Jessie's 16th birthday – she had a house party, we all did – in her parent's bedroom, while she was downstairs…

Sounds of pornography. SIMON kisses and gropes her but ALANA doesn't reciprocate.

SIMON: You're such a hot bitch. You're a hot bitch aren't you. Hot bitch. I wana put my fangars in your pussay!

ALANA: *(Grimacing.)* It wasn't what I would have picked. I only ever watched the soft stuff, where you don't have to actually see it going in and out, you know? But that doesn't count does it. Not like the stuff Si and his mates spammed each other with. Not like what he was showing me now. This was Proper Porn.

(To SIMON.) It's a bit, fast, don't you think?

(To the audience.) Not "but you're going out with my best friend", not "get the fuck off me you sweaty fucking porn weasel I wouldn't let your fingers inside me if you had cancer!" Just:

(To SIMON.) Bit fast. Yeah?

SIMON sighs, rolling his eyes, and goes to JESS, spinning her around and kissing and groping her.

ALANA: *(To the audience.)* But sometimes, when I'm feeling really shitty about things, I think "What if I'd just let him…?"

I started drinking. I knew I was embarrassing myself but I didn't care and Jess was just as drunk as me and somehow we – she – thought it would be a good idea to / …

(To JESS.) I can't.

JESS: You have to.

ALANA: I don't even want to…

JESS: Baby!

ALANA: Shut up!

JESS: I have some lube here somewhere, do you want that?

ALANA: What!

JESS: Might help. Make it smoother. As there's no flooow…

ALANA: *(To the audience.)* I wasn't even on my period. She just decided it was time for me to learn.

JESS: Consider it prep for your first big dick.

ALANA: Is this a good idea? I'm not feeling very dexterarous – dexrous, dexterious...?

JESS: It's a great idea. It's easy.

(JESS produces a tampon, presenting it to ALANA.)

It's tiny. See.

ALANA: Oh my god.

JESS: Relax...

ALANA: I can't do it. I just can't!

JESS: You haven't even tried. I've been doing it for ages and if I can do it you can do it. We'll do it together, yeah?

(JESS produces another tampon. ALANA hesitates.)

It'll be fine.

ALANA groans and concedes. They both cock one leg up on the bed.

ALANA: Isn't there a diagram? Where's the diagram?

JESS: Threw it out didn't I.

ALANA: I don't know what I'm doing! I need a visual aid!

JESS: No you don't you big tit, just think of, like, like a banana shape, with a weird balloon on the end. Like a tumour.

ALANA: Not helping.

JESS: Count of three. One. Two...

ALANA: I can't do this, this is all too weird and I'm too drunk I'm going to break something.

JESS: Don't be ridiculous, it's not a big deal!

ALANA: It is a big deal!

JESS: All this, it's all in your head. You're freaking out. Have you had something?

ALANA: I've heard they get stuck is that true? The string gets sucked up and they can't come out again...

JESS: Get it together!

ALANA: And what about Toxic Shock Syndrome!

JESS: *(Hauling ALANA back into position.)* One! Alright! You can do this! Two! Three!

ALANA shrieks.

JESS: Yaaay! That wasn't so bad was it!

ALANA: It's not… quite…

JESS: What?

ALANA: It just… touched me.

JESS: Maybe I should shove it up there myself…

ALANA: Fuck off!

JESS: Look! It's a little cotton mouse. And it's not going to hurt you. And if you don't get over this I'm going to tell everyone you're a frigid little baby who won't stick anything up her fanny.

They stare at each other.

ALANA: *(To the audience.)* Maybe she did know.

JESS: Take deep breaths.

(ALANA reluctantly gets back into position. She inhales.)

Make sure it's angled towards your back, yeah? Don't try and force it, it'll find it's way, just gently… gently guide it in. Just try and un-tense all those muscles. Calm them down, just relax.

JESS breathes slowly.

JESS: Well?

ALANA turns to face her, releases a smile.

ALANA: *(To JESS.)* Brilliant.

JESS: I'm so proud of you! How does it feel?

ALANA: Not so bad. A bit – tight.

JESS: Soon you'll forget it's even there. Now let's go see if Darren's got weed or if Josie's a lying cow.

ALANA faces the audience. She shamefully pulls the tampon out from her waistband where she has secretly tucked it in.

ALANA: *(To the audience.)* How could I have? She was right there.

That was the night I met Kevin. He was... good looking? I don't really know. And I don't really know how we met, or why he was there. He wasn't at our school. I think maybe he was older.

(To herself.) Was he...?

(To the audience.) Nope. Nothing. I just can't remember. I was – by that point, I was... I don't remember a fucking thing. But, I was determined. Don't remember what about, but I remember the feeling. Feeling – determined. I think that's why I drank so much, for some reason, but I'm not sure. Anyway we – somehow – ended up at his brother's house, in the spare room.

(To KEVIN.) Nice.

KEVIN: So like I don't know what you're up for tonight or anything but my balls are pretty fucking blue so I ain't got time for a tease, you know, I just don't got time for that / shit.

ALANA: I'm not a tease.

KEVIN: I wasn't sayin you was I was / just sayin...

ALANA: And I'm not frigid.

KEVIN: Cool, cool, yeah. Alright / then, well...

ALANA: Can we just get on with it? Just straight to it?

KEVIN: *(Beat.)* Yeah!

They get into bed.

ALANA: *(To the audience.)* He had a Sometimes Double. The bed, I mean. I always liked those, when I got my own bed in my first flat I made sure I got a Sometimes Double – more than enough room on your own and with someone else it forces a cuddle, or at least a spoon. But that's not what we were doing.

KEVIN reveals his erection to ALANA.

ALANA: I was wrong. This was the ugliest thing I'd ever seen.

KEVIN: *(Pleased.)* Yeah. You like that?

ALANA: I tried to give him a hand job. But it was like a sea snake, you know those toys? The water balloon that turns in on itself? Couldn't get, a grip, or… kept slipping out. So I just – because it seemed easier, that's all. And so I didn't have to look at it, I just put it – [in my mouth]

KEVIN: Yeah. Yeah! Yeah yeah yeah! Oh my fucking! Oh my yeah! Oh god! Oh yeah! Oh yeah! Yeeeeeaaaaah!

ALANA: We held each other afterwards.

KEVIN: That was fucking great.

ALANA: *(To KEVIN.)* Yeah?

KEVIN: Fucking beautiful.

ALANA: Aw…

KEVIN: I've like, never been this close to anyone.

ALANA: Me neither.

KEVIN sobs. ALANA comforts him, bemused but very very pleased.

ALANA: *(To the audience.)* I went home the next day buzzing. Jess was going to be floored! On the bus I got a text. It was from him.

KEVIN: Babe look I had fun yeah but if I'm honest I like you but I can't deal with this right now. See ya. Kev.

ALANA: *(Beat.)* I got over it.

(Beat.)

Didn't see him again.

(Beat.)

Didn't tell Jess.

(Beat.)

Let's see, what's next, um… Pete! I didn't know Pete. Very well. He went to my school. But we met – I say met, but there was never a "meet", just a sort of, final official acknowledgment. At school.

We went to a nice school. But there were these boys who thought they were hard. Never actually saw a fight. And their ringleader was a boy called Nathaniel. Yeah. And I remember standing in the cloisters one day and down the other end there was this younger kid, I think he wanted to take over Nathaniel's slot when we left, so he was practicing I guess and he was shouting down the other end at this guy who turned out to be Pete. I think he was calling him fat. Pete wasn't fat, but he was – soft. Rounded, not sporty, not skinny, you know? And Nathaniel hears this and strides down the cloisters like a soldier and looms over this kid and says:

NATHANIEL: Not too smart, what you just did. Pete's the best goddamn guy in this whole school, this whole town, and if you got a problem with him you've got a problem with us.

ALANA: Pete caught me there watching. I could tell he was embarrassed. I smiled at him. He smiled back, kind of because that's just what you do I think. He had nice teeth.

For some reason – maybe I just started noticing him more – we kept bumping into each other coming in or out of the toilets, or in the canteen, or in exams we'd clock each other. We still didn't talk. But he was in the audience at the school drama competition at the end of term. I didn't think he liked that sort of thing. Turns out he didn't, he was just – there to watch me.

(Beat, can't stop a smile.)

I won second. Points for my house, no real prizes. And honestly I think I would have won first if I hadn't been distracted because – what was he doing there?

Then the Easter holidays came and I got this really really long text. Do you remember when you could only use so many characters at a time and long messages would come through in chunks?

In the following "…" indicates a new text loading.

PETER: Alana, I've written this text because I need to say a few things to you. First and foremost I'm sorry about Thursday, I didn't mean to

…

ignore you but I did and I'm sorry, the reason I did is because people have been talking to me and apparently talking to you. I couldn't look at you simply because I was so

…

embarrassed, I didn't know what to do or say. I think you're very attractive and have an awesome personality and if you want to go out with me that's great and I would be over the moon but

…

I don't know if I could ask you out because you're so attractive and I know I'm no prize catch. Also you would be my first ever girlfriend and I would screw

…

it up in so many ways. I've never properly kissed someone and I've never dated someone I wouldn't know what to do and I know you've already had at least one boyfriend and I

…

wouldn't be good enough. I love you as I love all my friends and I think you're attractive but I would not want my feelings to get in the way of our friendship, if you don't want to go out with me

…

that's fine, I was not expecting you to, but I want us to be friends because I think you're great and I would never want to lose such a great friend. I'm eternally sorry for avoiding you on Thursday.

ALANA: I / …

PETER: PS I'm also sorry I couldn't say all this to your face I wanted to at least say it over MSN but you're at school doing the play and I don't know when that finishes and I don't want to interrupt.

ALANA: I / …

PETER: PS again my birthday is on Saturday. Do you want to come to my house party? Sincerely yours, Peter.

ALANA: … I don't remember him ignoring me. And no one had said anything to me, I have no idea what that was about. I should have texted back: "Pete I really like you too and this is the sweetest text I've ever had, seriously, how could I say no? Don't ever think you're no prize catch, you are, you're kind and nice and sweet and lovely and I'd love to go to your party on Saturday." But I just said: "I'd love to come to your party on Saturday."

(To PETER.) Hi Pete.

PETER: Hi Alana.

ALANA: Happy Birthday.

PETER: Thanks.

ALANA: How's it going?

PETER shrugs, nodding.

ALANA: … Cool.

Awkward pause.

PETER: Do you want a drink/?

ALANA: Yes.

(To the audience.) We drank, talked to other people, drank, watched each other from across the room while pretending

not to but both knowing the other was doing the same thing, drank, drank, danced a bit, drank, until:

PETER: I'm drunk.

ALANA: *(To PETER.)* Me too.

PETER: I'm sorry.

ALANA: Don't be sorry. Why are you sorry?

PETER: Because... Oh shit, I thought... I was going to, you know, kiss you tonight. But I was too nervous. And now I'm too drunk and you'll think I'm just kissing you because I'm drunk.

ALANA kisses PETER full on the lips. They descend into a long snog. PETER bolts and vomits on the other side of the bed.

ALANA: I have to ask you something.

PETER: *(Spitting.)* Yeah?

ALANA: Do you want sex or don't you?

PETER: What, now?

ALANA: No, I mean, just, in general.

PETER: Um, I don't know, yes?

ALANA: Ok.

PETER: Do you?

ALANA: Yeah. At some point.

PETER: Cool.

(Belches.)

Good.

ALANA: *(To the audience.)* And so we were a couple.

PETER: Does that mean we're going to Prom together?

ALANA: Yes, we had Prom at our school. GCSE Prom. It was great actually. I had my hair done specially and bought a really expensive dress and really expensive lingerie because...

(Smirking.) Pete booked a room. For the night. Of course we'd have to leave early, but it was exciting, to go to a hotel – all posh – it was all very exciting, all so exciting that I was sick in the lobby. In the toilets in the lobby, not in the lobby itself, not just on the marble or anything, I made it to the toilet. I wasn't drunk. I didn't want to be drunk. Not for this. We had this idea that we'd lose our virginity together. That night. We wanted it to be – American.

They sink down onto the bed.

ALANA: And it was all beautiful and I was ready and he was soft and warm and gentle over me and it – it – it was like, hitting a wall.

Ah!

A brick wall.

PETER: Um, it's not going… –

ALANA: *(To PETER.)* You're not hard enough.

PETER: – Is that normal? I am hard!

ALANA: *(To the audience.)* Like punching a grazed knee.

Ah!

PETER: Are you alright?

ALANA: *(To the audience.)* Like scraping… the back of your… throat…

ALANA passes out. PETER is very still.

PETER: *(Beat.)* Lani? Alana!

PETER shakes her.

PETER: Can you hear me! Oh fuck fuck fuck fuck fuck – Alana!

PETER tries to wake her, eventually slapping her on the face to bring her around. ALANA wakes up seizing, her whole body convulsing and shaking. PETER just holds her, terrified. Eventually she breaks out of it and breathes in big gulps of air, getting her bearings. They lock eyes.

PETER: What was that what happened what's wrong.

ALANA can't speak.

PETER: I'm sorry, I'm sorry, I'm so so sorry, I'm sorry / I'm sorry I'm sorry I'm sorry I'm sorry…

ALANA: I'm sorry I'm sorry I'm sorry I'm sorry I'm sorry…

Eventually ALANA faces the audience.

ALANA: *(To the audience.)* We didn't talk about it. And we both promised not to tell. We just… avoided it. Just kept on doing, other things. Sexy things. Just never inside. It was fine. It was nice.

(To PETER.) I don't know how you can bear to lick it.

PETER: I don't know how you can bear to suck it.

(ALANA shrugs, "fair point".)

I'm glad you do.

ALANA: *(To the audience.)* He was much more relaxed after that, funnily enough, more confident. Maybe he thought it was his big dick that did it.

GCSEs came and went and I did alright. And then I was in 6th Form. And everything was so different, I didn't have to wear a tie – Pete still had to – and I could wear jewellery – within reason – and I basically didn't have to do PE anymore. Well, I did, but I didn't really. Every Wednesday the last two periods were set aside for exercise and there was this gym in town we were allowed to use but it wasn't supervised and my mum didn't get home until way after I did, so we'd go to my house and fool around. It was aerobic! Pete had one of these – bionic penises. That could just keep going and going and I don't mean for ages at a time, I mean again and again. It wouldn't be too long after we'd finished that he'd:

PETER kisses her neck, strokes her.

ALANA: *(To PETER.)* Give me a second.

PETER: Alright.

He flops away.

ALANA: Oh not like that. Come here.

They spoon together. ALANA giggles.

PETER: What?

ALANA: Your willy.

PETER: What?

ALANA: I can feel it. Pressing.

PETER: Well what do you expect?

ALANA: It's not normal.

PETER: It's my gift!

ALANA: High metabolism is a gift.

PETER: Hey, I've not got much going for me but I've got this.

ALANA: Shut up you're perfect.

She kisses him. They snuggle closer. She squirms.

ALANA: It's in my back though.

PETER: Ugh, fine, hold on.

He adjusts himself.

ALANA: Argh! No!

PETER: What?

ALANA: I don't want your ball sweat on my back!

PETER: Ok, look, I'll push it down...

He does so.

PETER: There. Better?

ALANA: Yeah. It's in my bum though.

PETER: Not in.

ALANA: Between.

PETER: It's nice. Isn't it?

ALANA: I guess.

PETER: It, could go in. If you wanted it to.

ALANA: What?

PETER: I mean, I'm just saying.

ALANA: You want –

PETER: It's just a possibility that's all I'm saying.

ALANA: I don't think I – could.

PETER: Why not? Shit goes in and out every day.

ALANA: Pete!

PETER: It's true!

ALANA: Only out!

PETER: Well, same thing isn't it.

ALANA: This is disgusting.

PETER: Well, I'm just saying. Forget about it if you like.

ALANA: *(Beat.)* We could…

PETER: What?

ALANA: See.

PETER: … Yeah?

ALANA shrugs.

PETER: Oh my god really?

ALANA: … Yeah.

PETER: Amazing.

ALANA: Just… put it… against it…

PETER: Ok. There?

ALANA: Yeah – ?

PETER: I think that's it. Yeah. What now?

ALANA: Um, just – I don't know.

PETER: I'll just…

ALANA: Don't push.

PETER: No I'll just, let it, press… It's nice.

ALANA: Yeah?

PETER: Yeah.

PETER spits on her (between her cheeks).

ALANA: What are you doing!

PETER: I saw it – it'll help.

ALANA: I don't like it!

PETER: Sorry, do you want / some –

ALANA: No!

PETER: – … lube?

ALANA: … No.

PETER: Ok.

They wait in silence. ALANA's eyes widen.

ALANA: Oh.

PETER: Was that – ?

ALANA: See.

PETER: What that – ?

ALANA: Yeah.

PETER: Was it – ?

ALANA: Yeah.

PETER: Ok?

ALANA: … Yeah.

PETER: Ok.

They wait again.

ALANA: Ooooh…

PETER: Are you – ?

ALANA: No I'm fine.

Another pause.

ALANA: You're pushing!

PETER: I am not!

ALANA: Well, do then.

PETER: Push?

ALANA: Yeah.

PETER: Really?

ALANA: Yeah.

He pushes. ALANA softly groans.

PETER: Amazing…

ALANA: Yeah.

PETER: Do we need / condoms or…?

ALANA: Shh.

PETER: Is it – ?

ALANA: Just, go.

PETER: Alright.

He begins to move his hips back and forth.

ALANA: Oh my god.

PETER: Oh my god. Are you – ?

ALANA: It's fine.

PETER: Ok just –

ALANA: Don't, shh…

PETER: But tell me –

ALANA: What!

PETER: If I should stop.

ALANA: Don't stop!

PETER: Yeah ok. Amazing.

They continue to move together. They are both enjoying this. They moan a little.

PETER: Oh my god. Oh my god.

ALANA: Yes.

PETER: Oh my god.

ALANA: Thank god.

PETER: Oh – oh my – oh –

ALANA: Are you coming?

PETER: Uh – oh – y-y-yes –

ALANA: Oh my god.

PETER: Should I not?

ALANA: No. Go on.

PETER: Inside?

ALANA: Yes yes.

PETER: Oh my god I love you.

ALANA: I love you too!

PETER: This is amazing. I'm going to come!

ALANA: Come inside me! I want it inside me!

PETER: Here it comes!

He comes. They groan together.

MOTHER: *(Calling.)* Alana come down here!

ALANA: Shit!

(She pulls herself away from him.)

Stay here!

PETER hides under the covers. ALANA goes to her mother.

ALANA: You're home.

MOTHER: I heard everything.

ALANA: Everything everything?

MOTHER: Everything.

ALANA: Why are you home?

MOTHER: Bomb scare.

ALANA: Ah.

> *(Beat.)*

I'm sorry.

Silence.

MOTHER: Wait here.

> *MOTHER leaves. ALANA looks to the audience pleadingly. MOTHER returns with a packet of Microgynon.*

MOTHER: These are mine. We'll get you your own prescription but in the meantime – and I hope you used a condom?

ALANA: But / we…

MOTHER: But what. You don't want to get pregnant do you.

ALANA: … No.

MOTHER: So this weekend we're getting you pills and condoms and then that's the end of it.

ALANA: Thank you.

MOTHER: Well. Yes. You are…

> *MOTHER awkwardly dismisses her.*

ALANA: *(To the audience.)* I couldn't tell her what happened. What was happening. That I definitely wouldn't get pregnant.

We both got into Uni. Me and Pete. I went to Exeter. Pete went to Oxford… Brookes. He lost weight and I gained it. And the distance sucked but for the first time I was really, excited. I had a new page, you know, a clean slate. I could be, who I wanted to be. Who I was. And for the first time, I actually chose my friends.

SALLY: I can only come from oral sex. I'm serious, I don't think I even have a g-spot, I think it *is* a myth. Or you know like those people born with a hole in their heart? That's like me and my cunt.

(Beat.)

Wait…

ALANA: *(To the audience.)* Sally. I loved her. Still do. She was studying Art and Philosophy. She was really cool.

SALLY: *(Into her phone.)* Note: Hole in heart, hole in cunt. G-spot? Bullets? Possibly rats, with pierced ears.

ALANA: And she had a thing for taxidermy.

JOHNNY: That would make a great short.

ALANA: Johnny. Film Studies.

SALLY: I can't wait to move out of halls into some shithole so I can stop buying mice and start laying traps myself.

JOHNNY: I promise, when we live together, it'll be in the shittest hole we can find.

SALLY: *(Teasing.)* Not everyone likes their holes filled with shit.

JOHNNY: *(Playing.)* Homophobe.

SALLY: *(Playing.)* Piss off.

ALANA: *(To the audience.)* I was doing Geography and French with a module in Philosophy which is how I met Sally, and then Johnny. Pretty obvious I was there for The Experience. But it was an experience and these two, they… They were the best friends I've ever had.

SALLY: But you must have an opinion.

JOHNNY: How am I supposed to know? I'm not interested am I.

SALLY: But you're a queer.

JOHNNY: Which means I like queers. I can tell you if your brother looks good. PS he does, enough to eat, and anyway "A Queer"? Who says "A / Queer" anymore?

SALLY: But you're meant / to…

JOHNNY: If you asked a hetero if he thinks his mate looks good he'll say the same thing, I don't care how progressive you are.

SALLY: But girls tell each other how they look all the time.

JOHNNY: Yeah that's a girl thing.

ALANA: I guess if you've never been with a woman / how can you…

JOHNNY: 'Course I have!

SALLY: Who!

JOHNNY: Two actually.

SALLY: Who!

JOHNNY: My neighbour. And my cousin.

SALLY and ALANA laugh.

JOHNNY: I was confused. And I'm assuming neither of you have done it with the same sex.

SALLY: No. I've been so boring, but I intend to fix that by the end of first year. I have a list: I have never slept with a girl, a black man, an Asian man, any non-white basically. I've never had a threesome, or fucked anyone shorter than me, circumcised or with nipple piercings.

(To ALANA.) Have you?

ALANA: None of the above.

JOHNNY: Or buttsex.

SALLY: Or buttsex.

ALANA: / I've had…

JOHNNY: I'm circumcised.

ALANA: Really?

JOHNNY: Oh yeah.

SALLY: Are you American?

JOHNNY: What?

SALLY: Well you're not Jewish are you.

ALANA: Could be Muslim.

JOHNNY: *(Very camp.)* Oh yes darling, Allah and all that jazz, I love it it's a scream.

ALANA: *(Laughing despite herself.)* Johnny…!

SALLY: Well why are you circumcised then?

JOHNNY: It's not that unusual.

ALANA: It is a bit.

SALLY: Are your parents neat freaks?

JOHNNY: No, in fact it had nothing to do with them – what does that even mean? – I had it done.

ALANA: What!

SALLY: Why!

ALANA: When!

JOHNNY: This one crazy summer, when I was backpacking, and I went to all these festivals – all over the world it was so fantastic – and I just didn't wash.

SALLY retches.

ALANA: Johnny…

JOHNNY: You cannot shame me. I've learned my lesson and I am not that person anymore.

ALANA: So what, did it get – infected?

JOHNNY: More like invaded. Totally taken over, pillaged by tiny little mucus-making fungi and, other things.

SALLY and ALANA scream and giggle with gross-glee.

JOHNNY: So I said "Ok Doc, do your worst".

SALLY: Did it hurt?

JOHNNY: What do you think.

ALANA: And now you're – ?

JOHNNY: As a whistle.

ALANA: What's it like?

JOHNNY: It's fine.

SALLY: Is it less sensitive?

JOHNNY: It was more, at first. But now I guess – I don't know. Maybe.

ALANA: I've never even seen one.

SALLY: Yes you have…

ALANA: No.

SALLY: What about porn?

JOHNNY: Woah. Neither of you have had a trimmed cock?

SALLY and ALANA shake their heads.

JOHNNY: *(Getting up onto the bed.)* The things I do for love.

SALLY: Steady on!

JOHNNY: Just a poke about.

SALLY: I don't want a poke from a fag!

JOHNNY: I meant you, you bint! What, don't you want a look?

SALLY: At your dong?

JOHNNY: Purely research. Don't want you two out of the loop.

SALLY: Yes please!

JOHNNY: Well then be gentle. But. You did call me a fag which is way offensive so Lani gets first go.

ALANA: *(To the audience.)* They were the best years of my life.

JOHNNY has now undone his trousers and SALLY screams with joy.

PETER and ALANA are on the phone to each other. While PETER actually masturbates, ALANA just talks dirty.

PETER: What are you wearing?

ALANA: Just my panties.

PETER: Which panties?

ALANA: The purple ones with the dots.

PETER: Ooh my favourites. Are they clean?

ALANA: No…

PETER: What?

ALANA: I mean, no because they're wet. Because you made me wet. / Talking…

PETER: Oh. Yeah that's nice. Are you touching yourself?

ALANA: Oh yeah.

PETER: Do you want a hand?

ALANA: I've got a hand I need a dick.

PETER: I think I've got what you need right here…

ALANA: Ooh is it a big one?

PETER: How about you see how big you can get it.

ALANA: Mm ish sho big in ma mouf, is tu big.

PETER: Yeah, suck it while I rub you.

ALANA: Uh I like tasting it.

PETER: Your tongue feels good.

ALANA: I'm getting it deeper and deeper.

PETER: I'm getting stiffer and stiffer.

ALANA: I'm practically choking on it.

PETER: You're so wet.

ALANA: I'm so so wet.

PETER: I'm burying my face in you.

ALANA: How does that work?

PETER: *(Beat.)* I've changed position.

ALANA: Oh ok.

PETER: You're lying on the bed.

ALANA: I'm lying on the bed.

PETER: You're trembling under my face.

ALANA: I can't help it it feels so good.

PETER: I'm jacking off while I eat you out.

ALANA: I love it when you wank to me.

PETER: I can't help myself, I just thrust myself into you!

ALANA: Ooooh!

PETER: And I'm thrusting and I'm pummelling.

ALANA: Thrust me! Pummel me! You big cock fucker!

PETER: And I shove my thumb into your ass!

ALANA: Shove your – what?

PETER: Am I breaking up?

ALANA: Say that again?

PETER: Into – your – ass.

ALANA: So what are you fucking?

PETER: What?

ALANA: Are you putting your thumb in there with your dick or are you – what what are you saying?

PETER: What are you saying?

ALANA: Where is your dick?

PETER: In your gash!

   (Beat.)

   What?

ALANA: But that's not…

PETER: I know. We're pretending though, aren't we.

ALANA: Yeah but…

PETER: I mean my thumb isn't actually in your arse right now
is it / –

ALANA: Yeah but…

PETER: – you're not actually choking / on my…

ALANA: But you know I don't like it!

(Beat.)

How am I meant to get off if you're talking about – that.

PETER: *(Sighing.)* So, what, I can't even hope now?

ALANA: What?

PETER: Hello!

ALANA: I can hear you I just… what are you talking about?

PETER: Are we ever going to have sex, Alana?

ALANA is silent.

PETER: Because I don't know about you but it's a bit weird
being the only guy here who's a virgin. Technically. When
he's been with his girlfriend for three years. It's not normal
is it.

(Beat.)

We need to – figure this out. Because, you know, I've been
patient. Haven't I.

ALANA: You've – we've – We have fun though, right? What we
/ do – ?

PETER: Of course we have fun.

ALANA: Are you not – is it not enough anymore?

PETER: It's… I… look, I love you.

(Beat.)

I met someone last night.

(Beat.)

I wasn't going to tell you, because nothing happened. Because I love you. So much. But I – was tempted. Because – you know. And it's not every day someone comes up to me…

(Sighing.) I don't know what to do. I love you. I mean am I being / unfair?

ALANA: *(Lying.)* I fingered myself.

PETER: You what?

ALANA: The other day. I wasn't going to tell you. It was going to be a surprise. But I think I'm – ready.

PETER: Really?

ALANA: Yeah. I don't want to lose you.

PETER: I don't want to lose you either.

ALANA: I love you.

PETER: I love you too.

ALANA: *(To the audience.)* I took a train that night.

(To PETER.) Slowly slowly slowly…

PETER: Shhh…

ALANA: Sorry. Sorry.

PETER: Is that – ?

ALANA: Umm, it's not…

ALANA takes very deep breaths. PETER pushes into her and ALANA can't help but scream.

PETER: Lani!

ALANA: Don't –! Warn / me first!

PETER: My housemates will hear!

ALANA: It hurts!

PETER: I know it hurts! I'm sorry it hurts! What do you want me to do!

ALANA: Ok, actually, just go for it. Notnow! Just, when I say, ok, you just thrust it in, like a plaster, just do it, quickly. When I say.

PETER: Alright…

ALANA: Ready?

PETER: Yes.

(Beat.)

Are you?

ALANA: In a minute.

(PETER sighs and shifts.)

Just give me a minute!

PETER: I'm giving you a minute!

ALANA: I'm giving you my virginity!

PETER: Don't act like this is some special fucking thing because it's not! Everyone does it Lani! Everyone gets over it! You're not fucking special!

ALANA: *(Beat.)* Can't your housemates hear you.

PETER: Ready?

ALANA: No.

PETER: One…

ALANA: Pete!

PETER: I'm going to lose it…

ALANA: Ok. One… two, three.

PETER thrusts up into her and she screams again.

PETER: Shh!

ALANA: Get out get out get out get out get out get out.

PETER pulls out and off to the side.

ALANA: I'm not frigid. You know I'm not. I do / really want…

PETER: Just relax. Just… just sleep.

ALANA: *(To the audience.)* We somehow managed the whole night without touching. Not once. He had lectures in the morning. I woke up and he'd already gone. When I got home I had an email waiting for me:

PETER: Alana, I have a few things I need to say to you. First I'm really sorry about what happened, I didn't mean to snap at you, I know it was difficult for both of us but I did and I'm sorry, I just panicked. I really love you and I always have but I think we should probably split up. I still love you that's nothing to do with it, but I feel like I've grown up with you and really learned so much from you and now I need to do that on my own a bit because we're sort of staying still if you know what I mean. I would never want to hurt you, which is why this whole thing is so hard, and love shouldn't be this hard you know? I hope you don't hate me for doing this online, I knew if I did it over Skype or in person I would screw it up. I know that's not good enough. I still love you as I love all my friends and I want us to be friends because I think you're great and I would never want to lose such a great friend, but I hope you understand why I want to do this and I hope you'll respect that. I'm really really sorry, Lani.

Desperate, she darts up to her knees, legs apart. She rummages around and puts her hand up under herself. She struggles getting her hand in place. She becomes still, eyes wide. She closes them, breathing deeply, pushing the air out through puckered lips. She screws up her eyes, furrowing her brow, straining. She gasps and a jolt goes through her. She shakes her head again, inhales, winces, eventually must cry out, pulling her hand out. She hangs her head, shoulders tense, shaking from clenched muscles. She flings her head back, defeated. She wipes her eyes.

ALANA: The problem was me. Obviously. But more than that, what I mean is I had too much control, I was never going to do it when I could just say no. I needed to just do it.

I thought about walking through parks alone at night, hanging around dark alleys… waiting for someone who wouldn't take no for an answer.

Then I had a better idea.

Club music. ALANA dances.

ALANA: I hate clubs. The music – not only is it just bad, it's too loud. How are you meant to say anything, hold a conversation, how are you meant to get to know anybody? But then, I guess, that's the idea.

MARK dances.

ALANA: For example, we didn't have to chat for me to know: he'd do.

MARK and ALANA make out outside the club. They grope each other. She digs her hand into his trousers. He laughs. His laughs turn into a moan and then:

MARK: Woah, wait, wait!

(He ejaculates. Awkward silence.)

Don't worry. I'll be better at my place.

ALANA: *(To the audience.)* We managed to make it to his bedroom without incident and I even got him mostly undressed, but…

MARK has fallen asleep. He snores. ALANA sighs. ALANA takes out her phone and calls JOHNNY, gets his answerphone:

JOHNNY: This is Johnny, I can't come to the phone right now, unlucky! Leave a message if you like, but I don't check them, so BBM me if you really care.

ALANA tries calling SALLY and gets through:

SALLY: *(Whispering.)* Hi what's up?

ALANA: *(Whispering.)* Why are you whispering?

SALLY: *(Whispering.)* Why are you whispering?

ALANA: *(Whispering, looking at MARK.)* Because… you are.

SALLY: *(Whispering.)* I'm with someone.

ALANA: *(Whispering.)* Oh.

SALLY: *(Whispering.)* So I can't be long. I'm in his en-suite picking toilet paper off my flaps.

ALANA: *(Whispering.)* What?

SALLY: *(Whispering.)* Don't you get that?

ALANA: *(Whispering.)* No.

SALLY: *(Whispering.)* I do. I thought everyone did. Listen was there something specific?

ALANA: *(Whispering.)* Uh… no, just a chat.

SALLY: *(Whispering.)* You alright?

ALANA: *(Whispering.)* Yeah of course yeah. I'll leave you to it.

SALLY: *(Whispering.)* Ok great thanks, see you tomorrow.

ALANA: *(Whispering.)* See you tomorrow.

SALLY: *(Whispering.)* Ooh ooh Lani Lani Lani!

ALANA: *(Whispering.)* What?

SALLY: *(Whispering.)* He's Mexican!

ALANA: *(Whispering.)* Who?

SALLY: *(Whispering.)* My conquest!

ALANA: *(Whispering.)* Oh great, good, another box ticked.

SALLY:*(Whispering.)* Yeah and with the Chinese guy last week I feel much better about myself. Chinese? Or Korean?

ALANA: *(Whispering.)* You fucked him!

SALLY: *(Whispering.)* I'll check his Facebook page… Sayonara!

SALLY hangs up. ALANA shoves MARK so he rolls off the bed.

DOCTOR: Hello, sorry about the wait, one of our nurses is off sick and we're a little behind, so –

(Joking voice.) – What are you in for?

The DOCTOR gives a little laugh.

ALANA: Well, what I want to know is, I want to know if someone could just medically, surgically even, remove my virginity? Just put me under, break me in.

DOCTOR: O-kaaay, let's see, maybe. Why do you want to know that?

ALANA: I can't do it.

DOCTOR: What's the problem?

ALANA: Me, obviously.

DOCTOR: I'm sure there's nothing wrong with you, what I mean is, what's causing the trouble?

ALANA: No there is. I can't even get close.

DOCTOR: You know lots of girls have their first experiences later on in life...

ALANA: No I've had boyfriends, I've done things, I just... can't. I just can't. I don't know why, I don't know what the problem is, I don't know what's wrong with me or what I should do differently. Is there an operation so I can just get it over with?

DOCTOR: Are you talking about your hymen?

ALANA: If that's what will do it.

DOCTOR: *(Beat.)* I'm going to ask you a few questions if that's alright? They might be a bit embarrassing.

ALANA: Alright.

DOCTOR: Are you sure you're using the right hole?

ALANA: Yes.

DOCTOR: Do you wash thoroughly?

ALANA: Yes.

DOCTOR: Do you look at yourself, often?

ALANA: I have done.

DOCTOR: What about recently?

ALANA: A bit.

DOCTOR: Do you masturbate?

ALANA: Not really. Never… [inside]

DOCTOR: Ok, and so you've tried with partners, but what about yourself, on your own?

ALANA: Yes.

DOCTOR: And what does it feel like? When you've tried.

ALANA: Like… like there's something in the way? And it stings. Like it's raw, like there's no skin, just… it really hurts.

DOCTOR: Ok. It's probably Vaginismus.

ALANA: Oh. What?

DOCTOR: I'd like to examine you, if you don't mind?

ALANA is unsure.

DOCTOR: I don't have to go inside if you don't want me to, but it would be good, just to do.

ALANA takes a deep breath and lies down on the bed. The DOCTOR puts on gloves.

DOCTOR: Thanks, that's great. So Vaginismus is a psychosexual problem, it's when the muscles in the walls of your vagina spasm uncontrollably and cause a lot of pain and we happen to have a very good department for it here, so you're in luck. Plenty of people get over it. Now it may not be that, but it sounds a lot like it so I'd just like to eliminate the possibilities there's something physical causing you trouble, ok? Just spread your legs for me and move your feet up towards your bottom ok? Just so you're comfortable. Great…

The DOCTOR examines her.

DOCTOR: Great… Just a little pressure now…

ALANA winces.

DOCTOR: That's it. You're doing very well, this is great, really useful. Ok. Now I'd like to go inside just a little if you'll let me?

ALANA is silent.

DOCTOR: Is that alright?

ALANA shakes her head.

DOCTOR: Ok that's fine not a problem, not a problem at all.

The DOCTOR stands up and takes off her gloves.

DOCTOR: You can put your pants on now.

ALANA does so.

DOCTOR: Hard to relax, isn't it.

ALANA nods.

DOCTOR: So. A couple things, everything looks fine, very normal, just a few things that might be causing some problems nothing major. Ok, so everyone has a little bridge of skin at the bottom of the opening of their vagina, and that's usually pretty elastic but in your case it's quite tight, that's what that slight pressure was, just me testing its give, and there wasn't much there I'm sure you felt it. And that will probably improve with use but as you're not using it, it's not going to get any more flexible. And that's the first thing I'd suggest, is just to start exploring that for yourself and getting used to putting pressure on that part of you – go home and have a good look in the mirror, do you have a hand-held mirror? Just place it on the floor beneath you and have a good rummage, ok? Everyone's different and you're perfectly normal but that's your little difference, ok? Vaginismus is, unfortunately, self-affirming, so if you had some pain the first time you interacted with your vagina in that way the body remembers and the next time you try it's expecting that pain so it's a bit worse and sometimes the spiral just gets a little out of control and things end up being very difficult. It's nothing to do with you, you're fine. It's not in your control, do you understand? Am I being clear?

ALANA nods and can't help but start to cry. The DOCTOR produces some tissues.

DOCTOR: Aw sweetheart that's fine, you cry if you want to, it's all a bit much, isn't it. Me rabbiting on at you like that, it's a bit much, hm? Have a good cry, that's good now. Are you going to be alright?

(ALANA nods.)

Do you want to speak to someone? A counsellor?

ALANA: I just want to fix it.

DOCTOR: Ok. That can happen. It will be very straightforward, I promise.

ALANA: Thank you.

DOCTOR: No thank you. That was very brave of you to do, you know that? And you've done very well, no screams huh! I've had screamers! We'll sort you out, ok? Now, there are lots of options available to you. I don't think there's surgery that will help, and I'd much rather get you straightened out holistically anyway, and remember, almost everyone gets over this with time and a little work. So that's what I'd like to do. Like I said there's a great psychosexual department here and what I'd like to do is book you an appointment to meet one of the psychiatrists there, just an introduction, just to get an initial assessment, and then we can go from there. There's a ten step treatment plan you can go into, which includes counselling and graduated vaginal insertions – those are with little dildos made from a very strong glass of varying widths, and you work your way up. As well as these there's exercises you do with your assigned physician, as well as Kegel exercises you can do on your own at home, and of course no one's expecting you to accomplish this over night...

ALANA's eyes have glazed over a little. DOCTOR has moved away.

ALANA: *(To the audience, crying.)* She was so fucking lovely.

(Composing herself.) I don't know why I cried.

(Calming down.) I don't know why I didn't go back.

(ALANA lashes out, punching the bed in frustration.)

I'm sorry. Sorry. I just – I really hate myself because I should have told her – said something like "I'm sorry for crying, it's just no one else has spoken to me like that before, has cared so much about me, has been so tender when touching me and I know it's not professional but could I have a little cuddle because I feel a bit like you're my mum right now". I should have gone back and done whatever she told me to do, and stuck with it, even if it was hard and… scary. But I was feeling – it was all a bit – and I just went home. Had a shower. Watched iPlayer. A documentary I think. Fell asleep. Woke up. Watched the rest, the bits I missed, and that's when Johnny and Sally:

SALLY: Can we come iii-in?

ALANA: Yeah hi.

SALLY: Hi.

JOHNNY: Hi.

ALANA: Hi(?) What's up?

SALLY: We want to talk to you.

ALANA: …Ok(?)

SALLY: *(Beat.)* Are you alright?

ALANA: Yeah(?)

SALLY: Are you sure?

ALANA: Yeah I'm fine, why?

SALLY: Well it's just – we thought – … We know.

ALANA: *(Horror.)* What.

JOHNNY: I saw you. Coming out the doctor's. Red face and everything, so…

ALANA: I didn't see you where were you.

JOHNNY: Across the street.

SALLY: In the bushes.

JOHNNY: Figured it was something private.

SALLY: So what's going on? You can tell us.

JOHNNY: We're here for you.

SALLY: She knows we're here for her.

JOHNNY: Well she knows she can tell us too!

SALLY: Obviously she doesn't or she would have already.

JOHNNY: *(To ALANA.)* Don't listen to her. Do what you want. Tell us, or tell us to fuck off. But we are here.

ALANA: *(To the audience.)* They were my best friends. She had a hole in her G-spot, she'd understand. I could talk to Johnny about the buttsex! This was the perfect opportunity! This was my chance!

(To JOHNNY and SALLY.) I've – I've got… I've got a yeast infection.

JOHNNY tries to stifle a laugh. SALLY shoots him a look.

SALLY: Babe, that's nothing to cry about.

ALANA: I know it's just, it was just a shock. I'm very clean.

SALLY: I know you are.

JOHNNY: You are.

SALLY: Sometimes that's what does it though. Do you use scented stuff? That can give you trouble.

ALANA: Just Dove.

SALLY: *(Hugging her.)* Oh Honey, it's so unfair.

JOHNNY joins the hug.

ALANA: *(To the audience.)* I decided, fuck it. Forget it. You know? Forget it. This is how it's going to be. From here on out. I spent the next two years single. I lived like a nun with no god. Or at least, a god I hated. Graduated with a First. Left uni. Got a job. Stayed in touch with Sally and Johnny, worked my arse off and finally got my own flat.

A really nice place actually. With a little balcony and a fireplace and a Sometimes Double.

All to myself.

Just had to get the last of my stuff from my Mum's place.

ALANA takes out her phone and taps it.

MOTHER: *(Calling.)* You could help me you know.

ALANA: I'm just finishing this email.

MOTHER: *(Calling.)* Can it wait?

ALANA: It's to Sally.

MOTHER: *(Calling.)* How is she?

ALANA: Inviting me to her solo show.

MOTHER: *(Calling.)* You remember Jess.

ALANA: Yes.

MOTHER: *(Calling.)* She's pregnant.

ALANA: *(Beat.)* Really.

MOTHER: *(Calling.)* You can tell.

ALANA: Well good for her.

MOTHER: *(Calling.)* How do you know it's good news?

ALANA: *(Irritated.)* I don't Mum, I don't know, but I also don't assume the worst, I have a positive attitude.

MOTHER: *(Calling.)* I'm just saying! I'm just making conversation!

ALANA: *(To the audience.)* As if she'd ever done that before. I'd asked her to put everything in a box in advance, there wasn't much, it shouldn't have taken this long. In and out, job done. Should have known that was never my luck.

(ALANA's phone rings, she answers it.)

Hello?

(To the audience.) Telephone voice.

(To the caller again.) Yes it is.

Yes I just moved.

Yes actually I'm glad you called, that's the right address but I have asked you to stop sending them.

Yes I know but I don't have them.

Actually I have asked my GP and I...

Yes Doctor Simmons.

(Checks if her mother is in earshot.)

It should be on my file why I'm not having them.

Can you not just check the file please?

No I –

(Calls.)

Mum?

(Beat.)

(Hushed.) I have Vaginismus.

Yes, so I can't...

No, never.

Yes so it's very unlikely.

Well I couldn't have the smear anyway could I!

(Lowering her voice.) It just not possible for me.

Ok thank you. Thank you.

She lets out a frustrated sigh.

MOTHER: *(Calling.)* Alana?

ALANA: Yes Mum.

MOTHER: *(Calling.)* Um – where's the show?

ALANA: Shoreditch.

MOTHER: *(Calling.)* When is it?

ALANA: You wouldn't like it.

MOTHER: *(Entering with a box.)* I might.

ALANA: You wouldn't.

(Taking the box.) Thanks.

MOTHER: *(Keeping hold of the box.)* Have you been raped?

ALANA: What? No.

MOTHER: Have you?

ALANA: No!

MOTHER: You promise me?

ALANA: I promise I have not been raped! Why are / you asking...?

MOTHER: Then what's happened to you?

ALANA: Nothing's happened! I don't know what you're / on about!

MOTHER: I know what Vaginismus is.

(Stunned silence.)

It's when you're raped or molested and you're traumatized and / you can't...

ALANA: That's not, that's not what it is.

MOTHER: What is it then?

ALANA: It's nothing. It's fine, everything's fine.

MOTHER: Who were you talking to.

ALANA: None of your business and I can't / believe you were listening!

MOTHER: *(Breaking.)* Of course it's my bloody business you're my bloody daughter!

(Pause.)

Tell me what it is. Please.

ALANA: It's just something I had, and it's not a problem now.

MOTHER: You still have it?

ALANA: No.

MOTHER: You said you did, on the phone.

ALANA: I misspoke.

MOTHER: *(Beat.)* Fine.

Awkward silence.

MOTHER hugs ALANA, patting her on the back.

ALANA: *(To the audience, still hugging.)* It was a man hug. Pat on the back and everything. And it hit me. She was shit at this. Never was any good at this stuff. And that's not her fault. It's just the way she is.

I felt so sad just then, for a second, for her.

MOTHER: Was it my fault?

ALANA: No.

MOTHER: And you're ok now?

ALANA: Yes.

(To the audience.) I think she knew I was lying. Believed me anyway. I think she really needed to. So did I.

JOHNNY: This is fantastic! It's glorious isn't it! So edgy!

SALLY: What are you wearing?

JOHNNY: Too much?

SALLY: I thought you were going to wear my dress.

JOHNNY: I thought we were joking.

SALLY: I wasn't.

JOHNNY: You don't want a bad cliché walking around your show.

SALLY: Yes I do. What's the point in having gay friends if no one knows you have them.

JOHNNY: Why am I your friend?

SALLY: Go home and change, please. Please? For me?

JOHNNY: It's not your wedding!

SALLY: I don't believe in weddings, I believe they're an archaic patriarchal trap, so this might as well be. It might be the / closest I come to one.

JOHNNY: Oh my god fine fine fine fine fine.

(Exiting.) I'm a person. I'm a person!

SALLY faces ALANA and points to her own head, questioning.

ALANA: *(Reassuring.)* The show's great, Sally…

SALLY: Look while we have a sec, I want to say something to you, ok? What I want to say is that this is my night, yeah?

ALANA: Yeah(?)

SALLY: But you should think about it as yours. Lani. Now's your time. I can feel it. You know I feel these things. It's been a long time since Pete and you – and Pete was a nice guy but honestly he wasn't that nice and you need to let him go, he's not worth this, you need to get fucked. Basically. I'm not talking drinking I'm talking with a penis in your vagina, that's just what you need to do now. It'll launch you over that hurdle, get you back on the horse you need to ride. You know?

ALANA: Sally / I…

SALLY: You are sexy! You are so sexy!

ALANA: I'm / …

SALLY: And not in a conventional way, sure, and maybe that's why some people don't see it but I see it, I see your sexiness, you need to see your sexiness and run with it! Just have sex with someone, anyone, anyone here, pick anyone. Except for the guy with the grey bow tie because that's Morgan Twist and he owns a gallery. But anyone else. And just let them ram you, it's that simple. Ok? Just do it. Don't be scared. It's easy. There he is I've got to go.

ALANA is left shocked, frustrated, a little angry, and amused.

ALANA: *(To the audience.)* I mean, I love her, but sometimes…

ALANA catches GERRY looking her up and down. He looks away. She shares her disapproval with the audience. He looks at her directly. She realizes, looks back at him. He smiles. She questions him with a turn of her head.

GERRY: What do you think?

ALANA: About what?

(To the audience.) Had he heard?

GERRY: The "Art"?

ALANA: I like it.

GERRY: You do.

ALANA: Yes.

GERRY: You don't think it's sensationalist, vacuous and immature?

ALANA: No.

GERRY: What do you think it is?

ALANA: My friend's expression / of her talent –

GERRY: Ah.

ALANA: – and creativity.

GERRY: And sexuality.

ALANA: Excuse me?

GERRY: Obviously.

ALANA: *(To the audience.)* He had heard.

GERRY: Isn't it?

ALANA: No.

GERRY: You don't think so?

ALANA: Explain to me how a dead rabbit and some bashed-up butterflies are expressions of my best friend's sexuality.

GERRY: Your best friend is it? Well, it's about transformation yes? From a girl into a woman. The imagery is relatively plain. The Bashed-Up Butterflies have wings like labia, don't they, like thighs. And their abdomens obviously look like cunts. You're not offended are you good. The rabbit is the chase, the panting, the exhaustion, running down it's hole. And with its arms out, like so, there are clear references to religious ecstasy, pain and pleasure, rapture, you must know what I mean. And then there's the big wooden spike piercing through its soft, furry underside.

(Beat.)

I'm a curator.

ALANA: I'm frigid.

GERRY: *(Beat.)* I'm sorry?

ALANA: My cunt doesn't work. It's broken. I've never had sex and I never will. So actually, no, I don't know what you mean. At all. So.

GERRY: *(Presenting his hand for her to shake.)* I'm Gerry.

ALANA: Hi Gary.

GERRY: Gerry.

ALANA: Jerry?

GERRY: Geh-ree. It's Welsh.

ALANA: Ah.

GERRY: I'm not.

ALANA: Ok.

GERRY: Do you have a name?

ALANA: Alana.

GERRY: Alana I'm so sorry. I've been so rude to you. Let me make it up to you. There's a restaurant I know just around the corner. Let me buy you dinner.

ALANA: *(To the audience, shrugging.)* Free dinner.

The WAITRESS brings olives for them and they sit.

GERRY: Now I don't want you telling anybody about this place, any of the New Age Vintage Plaid Ironic Dickheads from back there. They'll ruin it.

ALANA: What's around your neck?

GERRY: India. Here, have one.

(Takes one out of his pocket and gives it to her.)

I give them to people who are, significant. And when I run out I know it's time to go back. You don't have to believe in it or anything, just take it.

ALANA: What is it?

GERRY: It's Amitabh. There are four Buddhas, each pointing to a different pole, and he's pointing to the west pole.

ALANA: There is no west pole.

GERRY: No, the western hemisphere, the western, the west.

ALANA smirks.

GERRY: They sell them outside this cave I go to in Ajanta. Inside is this enormous carving of Amitabh. Enormous. You have to climb this mountain to get there, it's a small mountain but it's not a hill. Couldn't jog up there, unless you're a fell runner like my son – runs up the bloody things, it's ridiculous, he's going to kill himself. Anyway you don't run but when you get almost to the top there's this opening – someone's carved into the rock with their hands – and you walk in and it's pitch black and you have to trust... well there's nothing to trust, you just have to go forward through this series of rooms all in a straight line. Your eyes adjust. There are the most beautiful carvings, ornamentation, bats. And the light from behind you starts to get fainter but your eyes adjust and eventually you see – his toe. That's it. His toe, as tall as you are and when you realize what you're looking at you look up, instinctively you look up and there, it, is. Towering above you. Carved out of the rock. Wonderful. I always get out, fall to the floor, and sob.

ALANA: Wow.

GERRY: It is. Quite wow.

ALANA: Are you bullshitting me?

GERRY laughs and looks at his menu.

GERRY: I'm starving.

Pause.

GERRY: If anything goes wrong over there they just make a religion out of it. I think it's very healthy. Born with five legs? Instant deity. You'd be a goddess.

ALANA: *(To the audience.)* It was cheap, and he was rude and arrogant and a hypocrite and too old for me and full of shit and not good-looking but not bad-looking and yet, I found myself sucking on those olives, very – suggestively. And checking in the windows that I looked good doing it.

She takes an olive, sucks it, looks to the audience as if there's a window and sees the face she's pulling – it makes her stop immediately.

GERRY: Would you like to go to bed with me?

ALANA: *(Beat.)* No.

GERRY shrugs and looks again at his menu. ALANA furrows her brow, trying to figure him out.

ALANA: I couldn't anyway. I said.

GERRY: How did you break your cunt then?

ALANA: I didn't break it, it's just broken.

GERRY: Right. That's remarkable.

ALANA: Nope.

GERRY: You don't seem bashful about it.

ALANA: Actually no one knows but you.

GERRY: I'm honoured. Have you never had sex?

ALANA: I've had sex. Just not, you know.

GERRY: Right. So you've always had this?

ALANA nods.

GERRY: It's really fascinating. Is it hereditary? Or a deformation?

ALANA: No just me being useless.

GERRY: Useless(?)

ALANA: Well it's my fault. Muscle spasms. If I could just relax them I could just get over it like everyone else does but no, I'm such a baby –

GERRY throws an olive pip at ALANA's face. ALANA is shocked and sort of smiling, but can't get any words out.

GERRY: Now, don't blink.

GERRY throws another pip at her face. ALANA can't not blink.

GERRY: See? Now is that your fault?

Long pause as ALANA tries to answer, can't, smiles, bats back emotion, clears her throat and says:

ALANA: Alright then.

GERRY: Hmm?

ALANA: I'll go to bed with you.

(To the audience.) And I did. A few times.

GERRY is giving ALANA cunnilingus.

ALANA: *(To GERRY.)* Oh, oh, oh, yes, oh, yes, oh yes, yes yes yes, yes yes, uh uh yes yes yes yes / –

GERRY shifts to glance at his watch.

ALANA: – oh yes, oh yes, oh yeah, oh yeah uh oh that's it, oh yeah, oh yeah, oh oh oh oh yeah yeah yeah yeah yeah yeah / –

GERRY pulls away.

ALANA: – what? What what's wrong?

GERRY: Ten minutes.

ALANA: What?

GERRY: It's always ten minutes in.

ALANA: What?

GERRY: Alana.

ALANA: What?

GERRY: I've had a lot of lovers.

ALANA: *(Beat.)* Fine.

GERRY: And I know what they sound like when they're faking it.

ALANA: I'm not faking.

GERRY: Yes you are.

ALANA: No I'm not.

GERRY: Yes you are.

ALANA: No I'm not!

GERRY: In fact I don't think you've ever had an orgasm with me.

ALANA: I'm sure I have.

GERRY makes a face, making clear she's just proved his point.

ALANA: I definitely have.

GERRY: *(A realization.)* Oh goodness.

ALANA: What.

GERRY covers his mouth.

ALANA: What!

GERRY: You've never had an orgasm.

ALANA: Yes I have.

GERRY: No, you haven't.

ALANA: Of course I have.

GERRY: What was it like?

ALANA: Really... really good.

GERRY: Do you masturbate?

ALANA: No!

GERRY: I think you should.

ALANA: I think you should fuck off!

GERRY: Alana, if we're not equal in this, then, then I'm a very bad man. I'm not – and don't want to be – a bad man. I want us to be equals.

ALANA: That's really selfish.

(GERRY can't help but laugh at this.)

Don't laugh at me.

GERRY: I'm sorry. Could you clarify your point?

ALANA: So you can still get off, as in Get Off, guilt free, right? Same difference.

GERRY: Whatever the difference if you're not getting something out of this then I'm not interested. Believe it or not.

ALANA: Well it is selfish.

GERRY: If you say / so.

ALANA: This is typical, this is so typical – I thought you were different you know! But no, it always has to be this way or that way or this thing and if it's not then you'll all just fuck off!

GERRY: Sorry? I don't / understand.

ALANA: It's always up to you! What you want! And I thought you didn't have any of that shit those conditions but it turns out you're just as picky as the rest of them you're just hiding it under this "concern" for my welfare or whatever and that's patronizing and you're not my dad or something you're not even my boyfriend and why can't things be the way they are! Why aren't I enough! As I am! Why am I not enough!

Pause. GERRY genuinely considers this.

GERRY: You don't want to come? You're not curious.

ALANA: Of course I –

(Sigh.) I don't think, it's possible for me, anyway.

GERRY: Why not?

ALANA: Don't you have to find the G-spot.

GERRY: No. If you'd masturbated…

(Stops himself.) I'm sorry. I didn't, approach this, delicately. I felt like a fool, I thought you thought I was a fool and I thought you were doing me a disservice but, I think actually, you've been done the disservice. And this might upset you, and I think maybe I'm close to understanding why, but I'm not comfortable continuing that disservice. I did enough of that when I was your age and an idiot. I'm not saying you're an idiot. But clearly you've slept with some.

ALANA: That is true.

He holds his arms open for her to come to him. She rolls her eyes and does, he settles with his arms around her, embracing her from behind – she is not on his lap. He takes her hand and kisses it, then places it between her legs. ALANA allows this, but from her expression she clearly doesn't expect much.

GERRY: I'm not going in.

ALANA: Good idea.

GERRY moves her hand in her crotch with her, pleasuring her. He closes his eyes and becomes very absorbed – ALANA steals a look at his face and it makes her stifle a laugh. She relaxes, smiling, sort of rolling her eyes at the activity. Then she notices something, her expression shifts to acknowledge it: a new feeling. Not necessarily pleasurable, yet. It grows. She tracks its progress. Then a spasm of surprising sensation. Another spasm. Her eyelids flutter, almost closed, as she submits to this rise of feeling. She moves her hips. GERRY watches her, responding. ALANA nods, eyes closed, little grunts. This all builds. She pushes GERRY's hand away, continuing on her own, until she comes quietly in his arms.

Beat.

PSYCHIATRIST: And that was the only orgasm you'd had?

ALANA: *(To the audience.)* Yeah. Until that point. Not anymore. After that we – as in right after, the first time…

GERRY's hand is hidden underneath her.

ALANA: *(To GERRY.)* … Are you – ?

GERRY raises his eyebrows and nods.

ALANA: … Oh my god.

GERRY: It was very easy. You didn't notice, did you. You're fine, aren't you. It's just there, it's just a finger. You're fine aren't you.

ALANA nods slowly.

ALANA: I'm going to faint.

GERRY: You're not going to faint, no, you're not going to faint – look at me. Are you. You're not going to.

ALANA: No. I won't. I'm not going to.

GERRY: No.

They breathe together.

GERRY: You're fine.

ALANA: I'm fine.

GERRY: You're fine.

ALANA: I'm fine!

GERRY: You're stiff, try to relax.

ALANA breathes forcefully out. This turns into a laugh.

GERRY: There…

ALANA: *(Laughing.)* Does this count as rape?

GERRY: I'll take it out if / you like.

ALANA: Don'tmoveit.

GERRY: Ok.

ALANA winces, whimpers.

ALANA: You're moving it.

GERRY: I'm not. Believe me.

ALANA: Oh I'm moving.

(Beat.)

It's ok.

(Beat.)

(Lip quivering.) Take it out please.

GERRY does so. ALANA breaks into tears.

ALANA: I'm sorry. I'm sorry. I feel – you know I just, it's like, I don't know but I'm – I'm you aren't I. I'm sobbing. Outside the cave. Oh god and I've got to do it again, go in again. I've got to go in because I've only seen his feet – his toes! You know? And I've got to go in and climb all the way up and how am I going to do that? How do I do it, how does anyone do it? How did they build it! Fucking – ! I don't know... It's not possible.

GERRY: It's possible. I'll help you. You'll climb it, of course you will, you'll scale it to the very top. And when you get there you'll look down through the pitch black and everything will be in light and you'll see how you got there and it will be momentous. And it's a gift, an honour to help you do it. To climb to the top and look down with you.

ALANA: Why though?

GERRY: Why wouldn't I?

ALANA: What's in it for you?

GERRY: *(Beat.)* That's not the point.

ALANA: *(To the audience.)* Weeks like this. I didn't go home, or to work sometimes.

During the following they alter the position of their embrace but never fully separate:

GERRY: How is that?

ALANA: *(To GERRY.)* Fine. Slower? Yeah. Ooh it's like it's creaking.

(Beat.)

I'm sorry I've just realized I'm gripping your balls but I don't think I'm going to let go because it makes me feel more in control of the situation I hope you don't mind.

GERRY: You can, grip my balls. It's only fair.

ALANA: *(To the audience.)* I didn't change my clothes, I didn't shower.

ALANA and GERRY hum together, eyes closed. Eventually ALANA breaks into a fit of giggles.

GERRY: *(Eyes still closed.)* This is a sacred meditation it is not funny.

ALANA: Yes it is.

GERRY: It's helping isn't it.

ALANA: *(Closing her eyes.)* Yes.

(To the audience.) Sometimes we shared a bath – he had a massive one with feet and everything and the taps on the side so it didn't press into our backs.

ALANA breathes like she's giving birth.

GERRY: I'm just there, I'm not in.

ALANA: Tell me before / you…

GERRY: I'll tell you / before I…

ALANA: Ask me.

GERRY: I'll ask / you.

ALANA: Don't go in without / …

GERRY: I won't. Trust me.

ALANA nods. GERRY nods. ALANA nods.

GERRY: Ok…

GERRY pushes gently. ALANA cries out and moves herself away.

ALANA: Oh I'm sorry.

GERRY: It's alright.

ALANA: I'm such an idiot!

GERRY: You're not an idiot.

ALANA: You should just give up, it's not fair on you, if I just give up at the littlest – we've done fingers, that's fine, that's all I need. I'm not going to be able – I'll never be able to / manage…

GERRY: Alana! I'm still here.

ALANA: *(To the audience.)* Sometimes he had to leave but we were together every night and every night we would try. Everything.

GERRY: *(Singing.)* The grand old Duke of York…

ALANA: *(To GERRY.)* He had ten thousand men.

GERRY: *(Singing.)* He marched them up to the…

ALANA: Gerry…

GERRY: *(Singing.)* He marched them up to the…

ALANA: Gerry…

GERRY: *(Speaking.)* He marched them up to the.

ALANA: *(Breathes deeply, moans painfully.)* Top of the hill.

GERRY: *(Singing.)* And he / marched them down again.

ALANA: *(Singing.)* Marched them down again

GERRY: Very good.

(Singing.) And when they were / up they were up

ALANA: *(Singing.)* Up they were up

GERRY: *(Singing.)* And when they were / down they were down

ALANA: *(Singing.)* Down they were down

GERRY AND ALANA: *(Singing.)* And when they were only –

ALANA: *(To the audience.)* Incense. Candles. Fucking baby oil, what a mess. Poppers – they made me laugh until I threw up. Nothing worked.

ALANA is convulsing in GERRY's arms. He holds her calmly, hiding his worry from her. Eventually she stops.

ALANA: *(To GERRY.)* … See.

GERRY: … Wowza.

PSYCHIATRIST: A syncopal attack. It's not a seizure.

ALANA: *(To the audience.)* Well that's a relief.

PSYCHIATRIST: Not enough oxygen to the brain, most likely from your shallow breathing. You're panicking.

ALANA: *(Beat. To GERRY, laughing.)* "Wowza?"

GERRY: What?

ALANA: *(Laughing.)* Who says Wowza?

GERRY: I do! And it was!

ALANA laughs loudly.

GERRY: Alana.

ALANA: Gerry.

GERRY: Where am I.

After a beat ALANA gasps and looks at him, surprised and happy.

ALANA: Oh my god. Wowza!

They laugh.

ALANA: *(To the audience.)* Nothing except… talking. Like I'd never done before, with anyone. And that, just that, felt really good.

GERRY: That's it.

ALANA: *(To GERRY.)* That's it.

GERRY: That's it.

ALANA: That's it. Oh god.

GERRY: You're doing it.

ALANA: I'm doing it.

GERRY: It's good.

ALANA: It's, ok.

GERRY: Do you like it.

ALANA: No.

GERRY: I can stop if / you [want me to.]

ALANA: Don't stop. Don't – just, finish.

GERRY: You want me to?

ALANA: It would help. I think. Positive reinforcement.

GERRY: I love you.

ALANA: You don't have to say that.

GERRY: No I don't.

GERRY comes quietly.

ALANA: *(To the audience.)* It went halfway in and halfway out and it took thirty seconds and I hated every moment of it but I did it. I did it. At 25 years old, a quarter fucking century, I finally lost my virginity.

ALANA exhales.

GERRY: How's the view?

ALANA: *(To GERRY.)* Just like you said.

(To the audience.) I owe more to him than anyone.

PSYCHIATRIST: And now?

ALANA: *(To PSYCHIATRIST.)* Um. Now…

ALANA positions herself on the bed as PSYCHIATRIST sits facing her, holding a clipboard with few sheets of paper and a pen.

ALANA: Sometimes in the bath now, if I slide forward, well, I don't really feel it then but when I sit back up again I really do – the water, rushing out of me. That's new. Very… new, very strange. And nice. And I don't like it. And I smell myself now. More like rain, I smell different. And sometimes not all the wee feels like it's out, feels gone, you know? I don't know what that is, is that just me? Maybe I'm imagining it, anyway, um, little things like that. Change, like that. Make me think – they make

71

me wonder... Gerry thinks I was subconsciously denying access to my inner spiritual and emotional worlds to any undeserving lovers, but then he would say that.

PSYCHIATRIST: And you're in a relationship?

ALANA: Well we still see each other. We see other people too though. I don't always have sex with them, you know, full sex. Sometimes I can and sometimes I can't. In fact, most of the time I can't. I still can't. Which feels, insane, irritating when I did all that... Weird.

PSYCHIATRIST: Weird?

ALANA: Yeah. It should be fine now, right. But it's just, not. So I thought, we could, you could help me with that?

PSYCHIATRIST: So you'd say your sex life was active?

ALANA: Oh yeah. Yes.

PSYCHIATRIST: And this, issue, doesn't get in the way?

ALANA: Yeah so when I'm with someone new I just say: "Look, I like you, and I think we're getting on well, and it wouldn't be fair of me if I didn't tell you –" and then I tell them.

PSYCHIATRIST: Is that difficult.

ALANA: Um, no, it's easy, surprisingly easy to tell them. And then I say "Feel free to run for the hills" but most don't. Most are ok with it. Most are thrilled I'm up for anal, so.

PSYCHIATRIST: And you enjoy what you do with them?

ALANA: Yeah. Yeah I, I come a lot more! Yeah I do. I just know, I know, you know, there's something missing.

PSYCHIATRIST: For you?

ALANA: For them.

PSYCHIATRIST: They've told you this?

ALANA: No, but... I mean, come on.

PSYCHIATRIST just nods encouragement for her to elaborate.

ALANA: I mean they're guys.

PSYCHIATRIST: Do you consider your womanhood, defined, in a similar way to their manhood? Defined by penetration?

ALANA: I don't know what you're getting at.

PSYCHIATRIST: What I'm trying to ascertain is – well, if I can be honest. Why you're here.

ALANA: I have vaginismus.

PSYCHIATRIST: Yes.

ALANA: And it's a condition, I looked it up, it can be fixed, by people like you.

PSYCHIATRIST: Do you need to be fixed?

ALANA: I have vaginismus!

PSYCHIATRIST: Who told you you need to be fixed?

ALANA: The internet!

PSYCHIATRIST: Do you want to be fixed?

ALANA can't answer immediately.

PSYCHIATRIST: Do you feel the need to be fixed?

ALANA: *(Frantic, confused.)* I don't fucking know!

(Beat.)

Sorry. I didn't – I thought – I thought this would be easier, be the end of it because I'd, you know, done it finally and, and I just told you everything I could think to, to tell you, and I thought you'd tell me now... what to do?

PSYCHIATRIST nods.

PSYCHIATRIST: The form you filled in, is helpful, thank you. But I'd like you to do a few questions again, with me, this time imagining that men cannot penetrate you. They're physically unable, you live in a world where no one is penetrated, ever, and no one cares. Is that alright?

ALANA nods.

73

PSYCHIATRIST: Alright.

(Reading from a form.) On a scale from one to five, with five being the most satisfied and one being the least satisfied, how satisfied are you currently with your sexual experiences, generally.

ALANA: Uh, without penetration in my vagina, right?

PSYCHIATRIST: Yes.

ALANA: … Five. Sometimes four, mostly, yeah I guess without that, five.

PSYCHIATRIST: On the same scale where would you place your sexual relationships?

ALANA: Four five.

PSYCHIATRIST: And your frequency of sexual encounters?

ALANA: Five.

PSYCHIATRIST: Your experience of pleasure during sexual activity?

ALANA: Five.

PSYCHIATRIST: I am very happy, Alana, to help you with any issues you are experiencing, any areas of concern, but if your sex life is satisfactory by your own set of measures, not anyone else's, then for us to put you through a program with the intention of normalizing your sexual activity, well I would see that as akin to SOCE.

(Beat when ALANA doesn't respond.)

Sexual Orientation Change Efforts, Gay Conversion Therapy. There is a danger here, which I'm keen to avoid, of pathologising your sex life. And before going further I would invite you to consider the possibility that your sexual activity may be different or unusual, but still valid.

ALANA: *(To GERRY.)* Everything has changed.

GERRY: Oh dear.

ALANA: In a good way.

GERRY: Oh good.

ALANA: I had to tell someone and I didn't know who else – it's like I have this new muscle and if I don't keep using it it'll disappear, it's like it's addicting – so I had my session.

GERRY: Oh yes?

ALANA: And it was fantastic. I just started talking, and didn't stop, and that felt sort of like a miracle because I'd never told anyone that stuff before but it felt really good to, you know? And they asked me these questions and said these things that made me realise I'd been thinking about the whole thing the whole fucking thing wrong, just totally wrong because I was actually really happy. Actually. I just didn't realise it. Because everyone was telling me what I was missing out on and I felt really shitty about it but those people are just like those Jehova's Witnesses you get at your door, who are really happy with this thing they've got but that doesn't mean you need it too and you believe in god and you're going to start going to church and everything! And it's not their fault, they mean well, they really think they're saving your soul or whatever and that's like me because I was in this constant state of panic and I was like I can't do it, What should I do, What am I going to do, but I realised, it's not that I can't. If I really wanted to, I could. I just, don't, want to. Enough. Anymore. It's just – not worth it. I can get off no problem without doing it, I do all the time now, so why should I go through all that shit every time if I don't want it. Just because everyone else is? Isn't that bullshit? And not everyone else is! There's this woman in America who decided she wasn't going to let herself be penetrated for political reasons and she's fine! And there's this other woman who had to create like her own vaginal passage because she was born without one! And she's fine! And there's all these gay guys who fuck each other in the ass and they're all fine and I'm thinking you know if I was a lesbian no one would give two shits about what I put up myself would they. And then my mind was totally blown I was just standing on the street, I stopped walking when the thought hit me that it's Just Not A Big Deal. And it's crazy because it was such a big deal for such a long time, everyone makes it such a big deal, and now it's just, not a big deal. For me. Now. After that session. And I wish someone had told me that before all this and I think you know this could actually help other people, I might write a book or a blog or something about it because suddenly, now, I don't feel wrong anymore. Or that I'm missing out on some essential, something. I don't feel like there's this big mystery, or that I've got this awful secret – it's like I've got a different sort of secret entirely, like I've discovered a secret, not that I have one. Do you know what I mean? Am I making sense? It's like, for me, I mean, I don't… I don't know what I'm trying to say. What I'm trying to say is, what I want to say is, I have no idea what to do now. Because it's not all mapped out. I thought it was, but it's not. And that's fucking brilliant. Isn't it.

GERRY: Fucking brilliant.

ALANA: Fucking brilliant. Fucking. Brilliant.

END